This book is dedicated to all who find Nature not an adversary to conquer and destroy, but a storehouse of infinite knowledge and experience linking man to all things past and present. They know conserving the natural environment is essential to our future well-being.

MESA VERDE

THE STORY BEHIND THE SCENERY®

by Linda Martin

Linda Martin, "a farm girl from Nebraska," is a graduate of Creighton University. Linda has spent 33 years working at Mesa Verde National Park. She continues to work there because it allows her to roam and explore the canyons and hidden recesses of the Four Corners area, and because of her interest in the Native American cultures in the region.

Mesa Verde National Park, located in southwestern Colorado, was established in 1906 to safeguard the most notable and best-preserved cliff dwellings and other works of a prehistoric culture in the United States.

Front cover: Cliff Palace, photo by Bruce Hucko. Inside front cover: Balcony House in late afternoon sunlight, photo by Bruce Hucko. Page 1: Pinyon Pine, photo by John P. George.
Pages 2/3: Long House on Wetherill Mesa, photo by Tom Till.

Edited by Mary L. Van Camp. Book design by K. C. DenDooven.

Tenth Printing, 2008 • New Version

Nature in Mesa Verde is like an artist capturing a cliff dwelling image or mood and preserving it for posterity.

The sky casts a glow on the pinkish-brown sandstone walls,
fading into a shadowy luminescence as sunset approaches.

The Mesa Verde plateau glimmers in sunlight most of the year, inviting people and animals to take advantage of the lush tabletop and canyon environments. Although most visitors arrive looking for the cliff dwellings they have read about in school, many are surprised at the variety of vegetation and wildlife awaiting them. It is little wonder that the Ancestral Puebloans settled here hundreds of years ago. The prolific natural setting allowed them to prosper for centuries. Life was secure enough that they concentrated part of their time skillfully crafting pottery, jewelry, baskets, and stone tools. They developed elaborate religious rituals still carried on by their descendants today. Their architectural achievements were amazing for a stone-age people. Mesa Verde is a living legacy of people and nature working in harmony with each other.

Snow dots the walls of Far View
House, a prominent mesa-top site offering panoramic views of the surrounding countryside.

The Mesa Verde Story

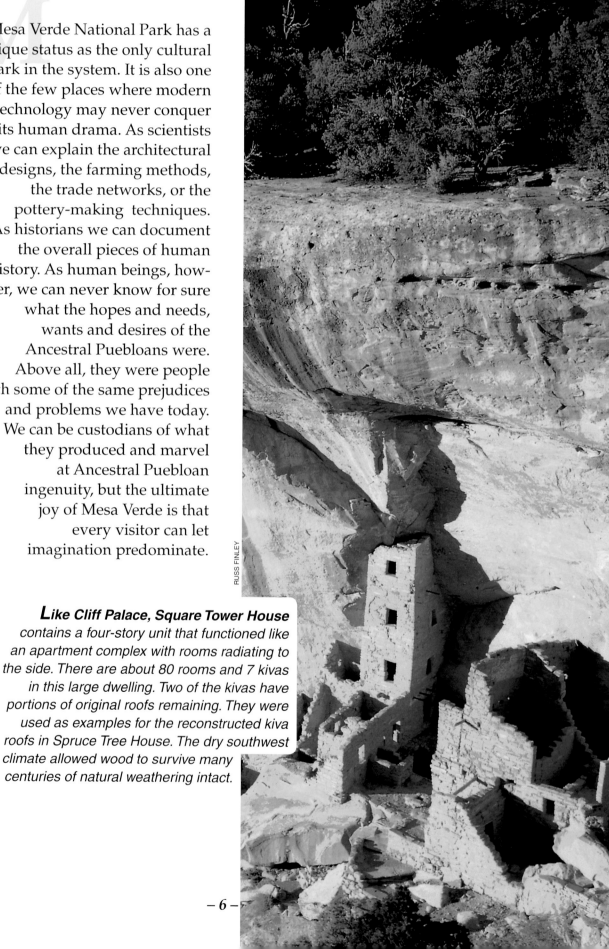

RUSS FINLEY

Mesa Verde National Park has a unique status as the only cultural park in the system. It is also one of the few places where modern technology may never conquer its human drama. As scientists we can explain the architectural designs, the farming methods, the trade networks, or the pottery-making techniques. As historians we can document the overall pieces of human history. As human beings, however, we can never know for sure what the hopes and needs, wants and desires of the Ancestral Puebloans were. Above all, they were people with some of the same prejudices and problems we have today. We can be custodians of what they produced and marvel at Ancestral Puebloan ingenuity, but the ultimate joy of Mesa Verde is that every visitor can let imagination predominate.

Like Cliff Palace, Square Tower House *contains a four-story unit that functioned like an apartment complex with rooms radiating to the side. There are about 80 rooms and 7 kivas in this large dwelling. Two of the kivas have portions of original roofs remaining. They were used as examples for the reconstructed kiva roofs in Spruce Tree House. The dry southwest climate allowed wood to survive many centuries of natural weathering intact.*

...every **visitor** to **Mesa Verde** can let **imagination** predominate.

Artistically designed Mesa Verde black-on-white pottery was shaped into mugs, bowls, ladles, and canteens. Its beauty is as admired today as it must have been in the13th century. Clay fired vessels were part of the everyday necessity of life. Making them into decorative pieces came later. However, when the people had to move on such necessities simply had to be left behind.

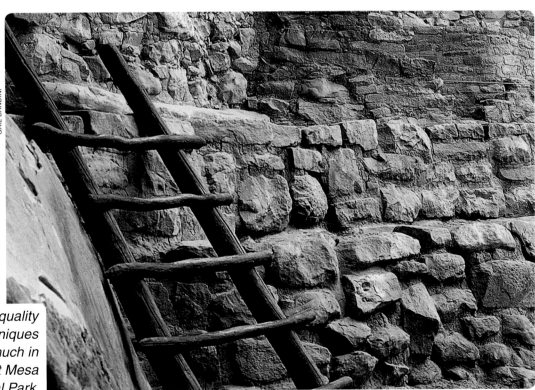

Here at Step House, on Wetherill Mesa, we find the blending of both the Basketmaker and Pueblo periods. Each level was built as a step back from the other below—thus the name Step House. The quality of building techniques is very much in evidence at Mesa Verde National Park.

*The years A.D. 1100 to 1300 mark
what is called the Great Pueblo Period,
the "golden age" of the Ancestral Puebloans
in the Mesa Verde area.*

The Ancestral Puebloan Legacy

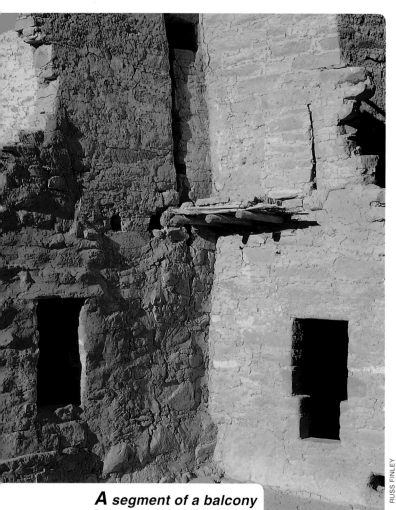

A segment of a balcony juts out from a Spruce Tree House wall. At one time, the balcony extended across about a 20-foot span. Ladders leading up to such balconies served as access to second-story rooms.

RUSS FINLEY

Cliff dwellings—ancient stone houses nestled in cliff alcoves and somehow shrouded in mystery— are almost synonymous with Mesa Verde National Park. Visitors inevitably want to see Cliff Palace with its towering walls and majestic setting. They marvel at the ingenuity of prehistoric people who were able to create such architectural wonders. Yet the cliff dwellings are only a small part of the entire Mesa Verde story. They represent only the last 75-100 years of a civilization that spanned centuries. Who were these people? What brought them to this area? Why did they leave? These are the questions surrounding Mesa Verde and its prehistoric culture.

It is frustrating for some visitors that so many questions about the Ancestral Puebloans remain unanswered. As a group, Americans are used to definite answers, expecting that scientific knowledge can unravel anything. Maybe the lack of written history is actually a bonus, forcing us to use our imaginations and conjure up our own theories based on known facts about why the cliff dwellings were built and what happened to the people.

The earliest inhabitants of the Mesa Verde region arrived around 10,000 years ago. They made a living hunting wild animals and collecting native plant foods. Archaeologists know some details about these people, although they left few remnants of their nomadic existence. After several thousand years of

Guided tours into Cliff Palace provide not only quality interpretation of the lives from 800 years ago; it also serves to protect the homes of these Ancestral Puebloans.

BRUCE HUCKO

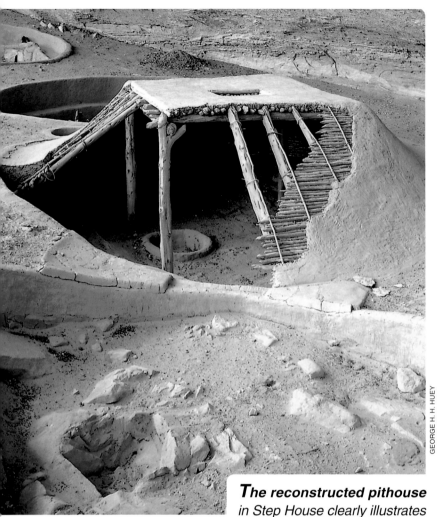

*T*he reconstructed pithouse *in Step House clearly illustrates roof construction during Modified Basketmaker times. A thick layer of mud on the outside helped insulate against the elements, keeping people dry and fairly cozy.*

GEORGE H. H. HUEY

Although there is no record of what the ancient people called themselves, the term Ancestral Puebloans is used to refer to them. This term replaces the Navajo word Anasazi, which for years appeared in all the literature. Modern descendants believe that Ancestral Puebloans more accurately describes their ancestors.

When they left this area, the Ancestral Puebloans migrated south into what is now New Mexico and Arizona, settling in the Rio Grande pueblos, Acoma, Zuni, and the Hopi mesas. Over the years their descendants assimilated into these groups. For this reason archaeologists use modern Pueblo practices to help analyze archaeological sites and answer questions about them. Rangers remind visitors of this when they take a tour of a dwelling.

Modern Pueblo society is often clan oriented, consisting of related families descended from common ancestors. Unlike Europeans, who trace their ancestry through the father's side of the family (patrilineal), most Pueblos trace their line of descent through the women (matrilineal). Ancestral Puebloan families were also probably matrilineal with women owning the houses as well as the property inside them. When a couple married, the man moved into his wife's house and joined her relatives.

hunting and gathering, they began adopting a more settled lifestyle.

This transition emerged because of two major factors: the building of permanent living and storage structures, and the cultivation of gardens (horticulture) and domestication of plants. Once people began leading an agricultural way of life, changes in their cultural and social habits soon followed. In the Four Corners area of the southwestern United States this way of life was called the Ancestral Puebloan cultural tradition.

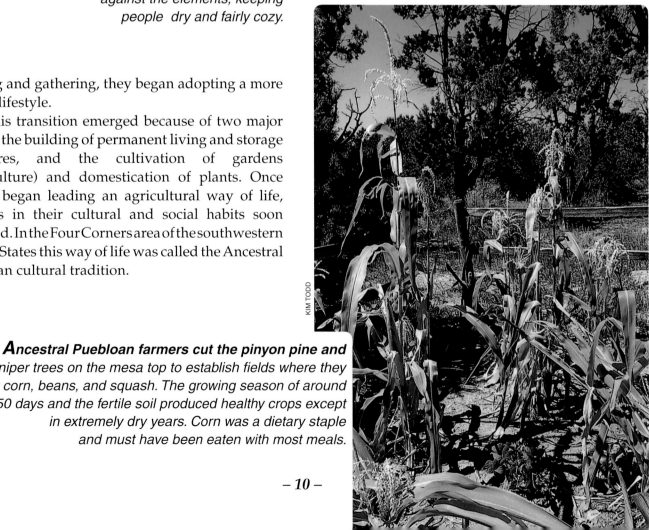

*A*ncestral Puebloan farmers cut the pinyon pine and *juniper trees on the mesa top to establish fields where they grew corn, beans, and squash. The growing season of around 150 days and the fertile soil produced healthy crops except in extremely dry years. Corn was a dietary staple and must have been eaten with most meals.*

KIM TODD

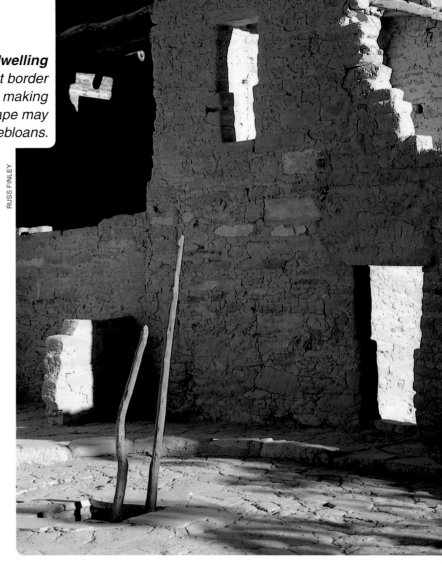

***T*-shaped doorways are a common feature in cliff dwelling** *architecture. They are usually found in walls that border courtyards. They may have served a practical purpose, making movement in and out of a room easier, or the "T" shape may have had some symbolic meaning to the Ancestral Puebloans.*

Similar customs applied to religious and ceremonial activities. Important elements in their lives revolved around hunting, farming in a fairly marginal environment, and praying for rain and fertility. Their gods must have made sure that plants, animals, and water were available for daily existence. These are important concepts to keep in mind when considering the Mesa Verde Ancestral Puebloans.

There are always visitor questions about the size of the Ancestral Puebloans. An average man was 5'4" to 5'5" tall, while an average woman was 5' to 5'1". Burials reveal that they had straight black hair, often cropped short for the women. They had muscular bodies adapted to the vigorous activity of their daily lives. An average lifespan was fairly short—about 32-34 years—although some people lived into their 40s and 50s. Infant mortality was high; about 50 percent of the children died before they reached the age of five. Women typically lived shorter lives than men because of childbearing difficulties. These statistics seem strange to visitors, yet Europeans of that time period averaged the same size and lived about the same length of time.

Causes of death for the Ancestral Puebloans ranged from arthritis and rheumatism to poor sanitary conditions and tooth decay. Skeletal remains often show teeth worn to the nub from chewing, or a lack of teeth completely. Such people may have pulled cavity-ridden teeth to eliminate pain and suffering. Dietary deficiencies such as iron were common. Some people endured bone deformities which made movement painful. All of these difficulties were typical considering the type of lifestyle they led.

THE BASKETMAKER TRADITION

The earliest Ancestral Puebloans excelled in the art of basketry, they are known as "Basketmakers." Many of their baskets were so finely woven that they would hold water. They also wove intricate sandals made of yucca fibers. The Basketmakers hunted with a throwing spear called an atlatl, and gathered seeds, nuts, and berries. They often lived in shallow rock shelters where they stored food in stone-lined cysts. Archaeologists have not located any early Basketmaker sites in the park.

By A.D. 550, the Modified Basketmaker Period began, coinciding with Mesa Verde occupation in cliff alcoves and on the mesa top. Modified Basketmakers continued to make baskets, but they learned a new concept vital to their cultural development—the making of pottery. Pottery made food processing and cooking not only easier, but also more efficient.

The Ancestral Puebloans built semi-subterranean dwellings called pithouses on the mesa top and in alcoves. Agriculture developed with the growth of corn, beans, and squash, the three staple crops of the Southwest. They replaced the atlatl with the bow and arrow, allowing them to hunt with greater efficiency. They domesticated turkeys, using them as a source of food and feathers. Although pithouse sites are not as impressive as cliff dwellings, this period laid the foundations for the flourishing farming tradition which visitors find so remarkable today.

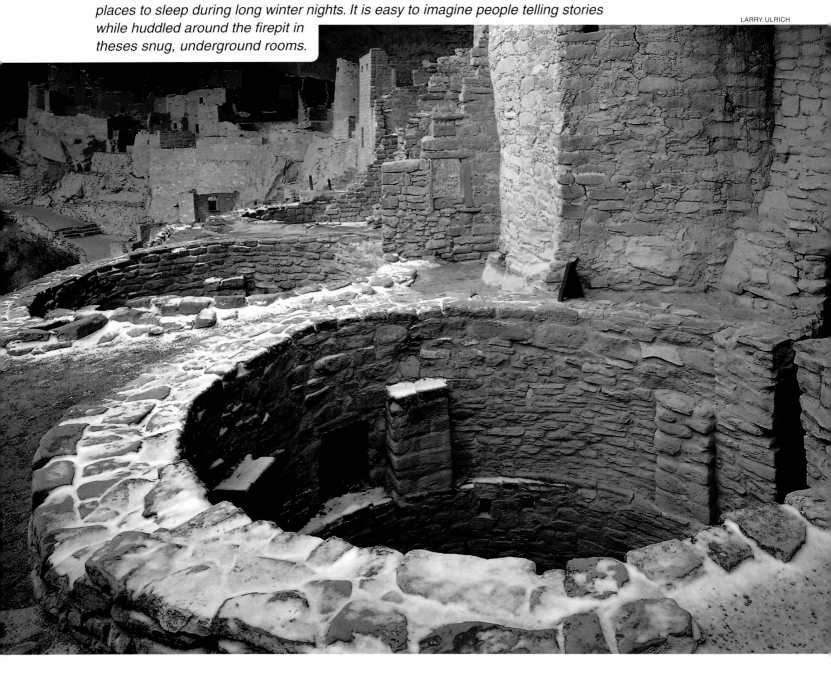

Cliff alcoves were cold and miserable places during the winter months, when days were short and temperatures dropped to zero or below overnight. Snowstorms made movement difficult, yet examples of Ancestral Puebloan snowshoes exist. Perhaps the kivas were favorite places to sleep during long winter nights. It is easy to imagine people telling stories while huddled around the firepit in theses snug, underground rooms.

LARRY ULRICH

Pueblo Occupation

Around A.D. 750, the Ancestral Puebloans began replacing their pithouses with surface dwellings, and a new era in construction began. The Developmental Pueblo Period is characterized by rows of connected rooms with vertical walls and flat roofs. In front of these L- or U-shaped houses the Ancestral Puebloans dug deep pit rooms, separating the architectural structure into an above-ground and a below-ground unit.

The underground rooms later evolved into ceremonial structures known by the Hopi word "kiva." Surface houses developed into masonry units using sandstone blocks and mud mortar. These architectural achievements signaled that a more formalized kinship and religious system had evolved.

One interesting aspect of Developmental Pueblo living was the change in cradleboards. They were soft and padded in the Modified Basketmaker Period, protecting the infant's head. In contrast, the new cradleboards were hard, causing a flattening of the baby's head and broadening of the face. Who knows—maybe fashion-conscious Ancestral Puebloans thought this made them more beautiful!

Pottery-making techniques continued to improve throughout the Developmental Pueblo Period. In fact, pottery analysis is one way archaeologists can date Ancestral Puebloan occupation. Changes in detail and design enable them to trace cultural development. In the late Developmental Pueblo Period, for example, the Ancestral Puebloans began making corrugated pottery for kitchen use. On such pots they pinched the surface with their fingers to give the clay a rough texture. Visitors can see the changes in the distinctive Mesa Verde black-on-white and corrugated pottery in exhibits at the Chapin Mesa Archeological Museum.

Neither Modified Basketmakers nor Developmental Puebloans led an isolated existence. Even though they had to travel on foot, there is evidence of elaborate trade networks. Excavations reveal red pottery with black designs—a color the local clay would not produce. The Ancestral Puebloans wove cotton textiles, yet the Mesa Verde climate is not conducive to the growth of cotton. It had to have been brought in through trade with people in northern Arizona.

Most turquoise found in Mesa Verde originally came from the Cerrillos Hills between Santa Fe and Albuquerque, New Mexico. Shell beads and bracelets came from as far as the Gulf of California. Undoubtedly, ideas were also exchanged. The Ancestral Puebloans must have had as much curiosity about other people and their customs as we do today.

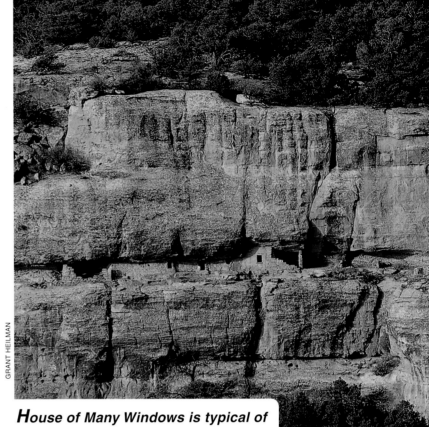

GRANT HEILMAN

House of Many Windows is typical of small cliff dwellings. Tucked into precarious alcoves not easily accessible, such dwellings are scattered up and down the canyons of Mesa Verde. This dwelling contained about 15 rooms, housing 15-20 people. The Ancestral Puebloans traveled to the mesa top daily.

THE GREAT PUEBLO PERIOD

The years A.D. 1100 to 1300 mark what is called the Great Pueblo Period, the "golden age" of the Ancestral Puebloans in the Mesa Verde area. There were no radical changes which inaugurated this period, but rather a refining of cultural elements arising out of the earlier periods. Probably the most notable cause for this cultural climax is perfection of agricultural skills. Using improved varieties of corn, the Ancestral Puebloans could increase their yields. They had already developed check dams in drainages where additional crops could be grown. By increasing the amount of arable land, the Ancestral Puebloans could concentrate more time on projects involving arts and crafts, religion, and social organization.

During the Great Pueblo Period the Ancestral Puebloans moved from small, scattered villages all over the mesa tops to larger, more compact communities. Often dwellings became multi-storied structures, as many as four stories high. Kivas, which had been located in the open away from house units, began to be incorporated within the walls of the village itself. Kiva roofs formed enclosed plazas where work could be concentrated. Stone towers, sometimes connected to a kiva by a tunnel, may have been built for lookout or signaling purposes or some symbolic religious belief. Towers located in prominent positions certainly afforded excellent views of the surrounding countryside.

In earlier times stones used in house construction were rough-hewn and unevenly shaped. Some sites did contain wedge-shaped stones chipped fairly evenly, but Great Pueblo Period builders increasingly made rectangular stones of a uniform size. They chipped and shaped the stones, pecking the surface to create a dimpled effect. These stones were pleasing to the eye—a craftsman's delight! They required less mortar to hold them together. Within the mortar the Ancestral Puebloans placed little chinking stones to fill in gaps and alleviate cracking. Clearly, the architectural construction epitomized by Sun Temple was the hallmark of Mesa Verde builders.

In the late 1190s and early 1200s, the Ancestral Puebloans began constructing the cliff dwellings for which Mesa Verde is famous. Why they built giants such as Cliff Palace and Long House, no one really knows. The sheltering alcoves provided relief from

Ancestral Puebloan stonework varies from crude to truly elaborate. Skilled craftsmen gave some walls smooth, finished texture, while others indicated shoddy workmanship—human nature at work!

wind, rain, and snow, avoiding the effects of climate. Some researchers believe cliff dwellings were defensive structures protecting people from each other or invading enemies. There may have been religious or emotional motives for building in the cliffs. For whatever reasons, most people moved into the cliffs, although some stayed in mesa-top villages such as Far View.

Of the almost 5,000 sites in Mesa Verde National Park, only about 600 are cliff dwellings. Most visitors arrive with the impression that all cliff dwellings are large units such as Spruce Tree House and Cliff Palace. However, the vast majority are small, containing fewer than 20 rooms each.

There is a high ratio of kivas to living rooms in the large sites, yet most of the small ones have no kivas at all. The dwellings face various directions, indicating that the Ancestral Puebloans used whatever alcove was available. Some have water sources in them, while others required carrying water from nearby springs.

In front of or below cliff dwellings archaeologists find refuse or trash heaps. Materials such as broken pottery, bone or stone tools, discarded yucca fiber sandals, worn-out clothing, cold ashes from fires, human waste, and a variety of corn cobs, squash, and other food were all thrown in these areas. Archaeological excavators sift through these trash

heaps in an attempt to locate materials for reconstructing information about the daily lives of the Ancestral Puebloans. These trash slopes enable them to answer many questions that would otherwise remain a mystery.

The Ancestral Puebloans commonly buried their dead in these refuse areas. This practice had nothing to do with any dishonor or disrespect; the loose material was probably much easier to dig than the surrounding ground, especially during the winter months when it was frozen. The body was usually buried in a flexed position with the knees drawn up to the chest and wrapped in a yucca-fiber mat, rabbit-fur robe, or turkey-feather blanket.

Objects such as pottery and tools, which might be considered useful in the next life, were buried with the individual. Jewelry and ornaments were other typical possessions placed on the bodies.

The solitary winter visitor sees the alcoves framed in snow—a picture worth a thousand words. Those who take a morning tour of Spruce Tree House find out how cold and miserable the alcoves can be. It is easy to imagine the Ancestral Puebloans huddled around fires, dressed in skins and hides, and using turkey-feather blankets to keep warm. It is equally easy to idealize these talented people, yet theirs was a harsh life with many of the same pitfalls facing people today.

Mesa-top sites such as Pipe Shrine House appear picturesque covered in snow. However, the winter visitor who trudges through the snow quickly learns how difficult it was for the Ancestral Puebloans. Clay pipes excavated from one of the rooms gave the dwelling its name.

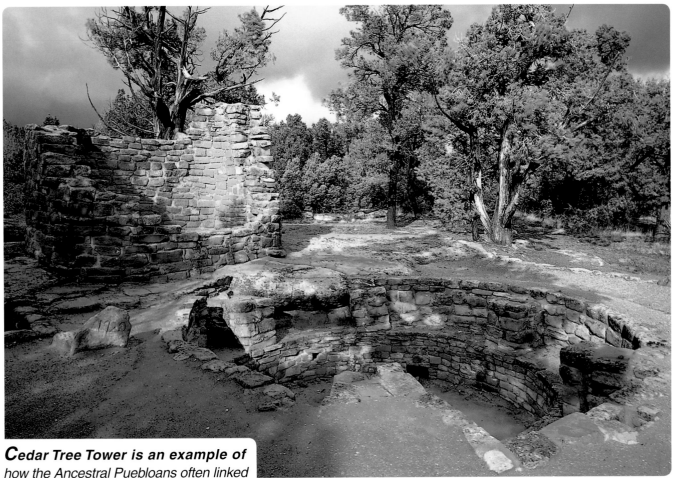

Cedar Tree Tower is an example of how the Ancestral Puebloans often linked a tower to a kiva. Perhaps the tunnel to the kiva allowed them to signal people inside of approaching danger. Archaeologists are uncertain if there was a threat or an entirely different reason for the connection. Note fire scene on pages 42-43.

JOHN P. GEORGE

ABANDONMENT OF MESA VERDE

Why did the Ancestral Puebloans build such massive dwellings only to leave them in less than 100 years? In the late 1200s there was a serious drought which must have taken a toll on harvests and productivity, and so good farmland may have been depleted. A cooling-off period, almost like a mini-ice age, could have shortened the growing season and prevented the Ancestral Puebloans from continuing as successful farmers.

In addition, the peak of population occurred in the later years. Perhaps too many people competed for available natural resources. They may have heard of the dynamic communities to the south were flourishing, and so drawn to such places.

For whatever reasons, the Ancestral Puebloans migrated out of the area over a 25- to 50-year span. It was not a massive migration but rather a slow movement southward. The former splendor of the cliff dwellings deteriorated with the ravages of time. Only the spirit of the Ancestral Puebloans remains.

RECENT ARCHITECTURAL RESEARCH

Archaeologists have recently been using architectural documentation in a few of the cliff dwellings to learn more about the Ancestral Puebloan people without digging in the sites. This multilevel approach presumes that a people's architecture can tell a lot about their social organization, providing a better understanding of how these people lived on a regular basis. This documentation includes mapping the site, recording architectural details, determining the building sequence of the site using tree-ring dates combined with wall alignments, defining household units and room functions, and recording historical stabilization.

SUGGESTED READING

CORDELL, LINDA. *Ancient Pueblo Peoples.* Montreal and Washington, D.C.: St. Remy Press and Smithsonian Books, 1994.

FIERO, KATHLEEN. *Balcony House: A History of a Cliff Dwelling.* Mesa Verde, Colorado: Mesa Verde Museum Association, 1999.

NOBLE, DAVID GRANT (ED.). *The Mesa Verde World.* Santa Fe, New Mexico: The School of American Research Press, 2006.

Far View and Sun Temple

The Far View area consists of a series of mesa-top dwellings occupied from the A.D. 900s until the abandonment of Mesa Verde. The double course masonry walls are composed of finely shaped stones held together by mud mortar. Lintels over doorways were either stone slabs or pieces of wood set into the surrounding sandstone blocks. Today these walls are heavily stabilized to withstand severe weather conditions. A few of the kivas are larger and deeper than those in cliff dwellings. What a chore it must have been to chop down enough trees to roof over so many kivas and rooms. No wonder the Ancestral Puebloans used up many of their timber resources!

TERRY DONNELLY

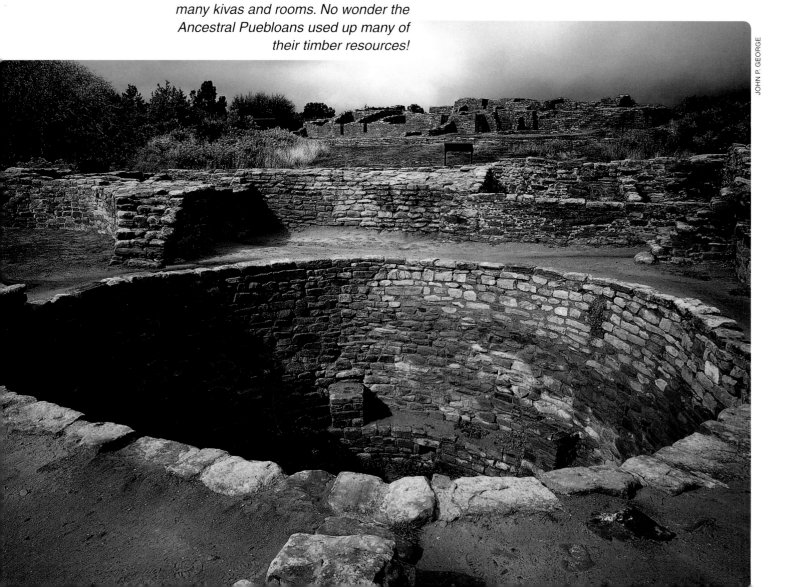

JOHN P. GEORGE

Only the Spirit of the Ancestral Puebloans Remains.

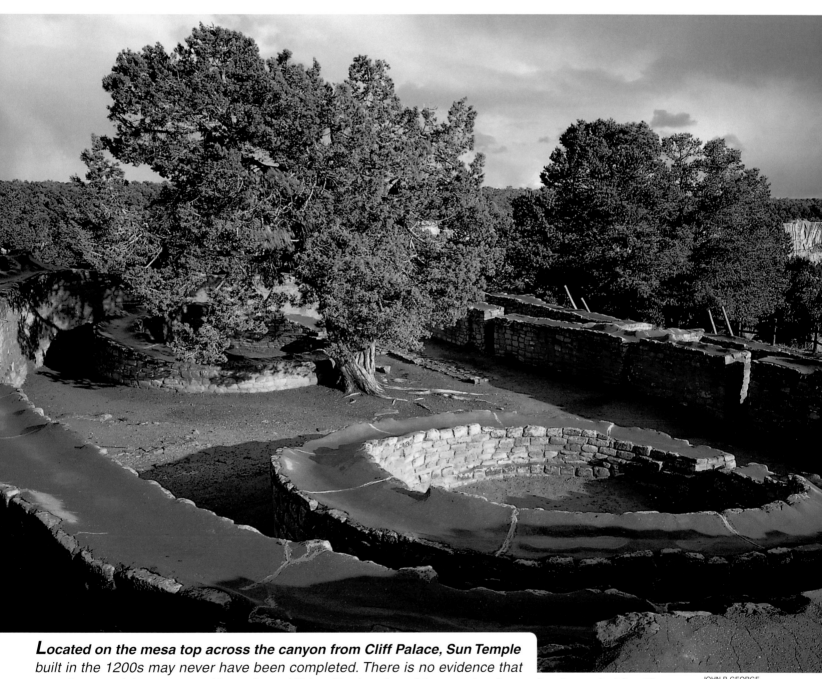

JOHN P. GEORGE

Located on the mesa top across the canyon from Cliff Palace, Sun Temple built in the 1200s may never have been completed. There is no evidence that a roof covered the rooms or kivas. Jesse Walter Fewkes found few potsherds or other household artifacts during the excavation of this D-shaped dwelling in 1915. Archaeologists believe it may have been a ceremonial structure of a large community. No other mesa-top dwelling is enclosed by double walls with long, narrow rooms between them. The stones making up the walls are shaped by pecking. Fewkes put a concrete capping on the walls to prevent deterioration from rain and snow which would erode the mud mortar in the walls.

Cliff Palace

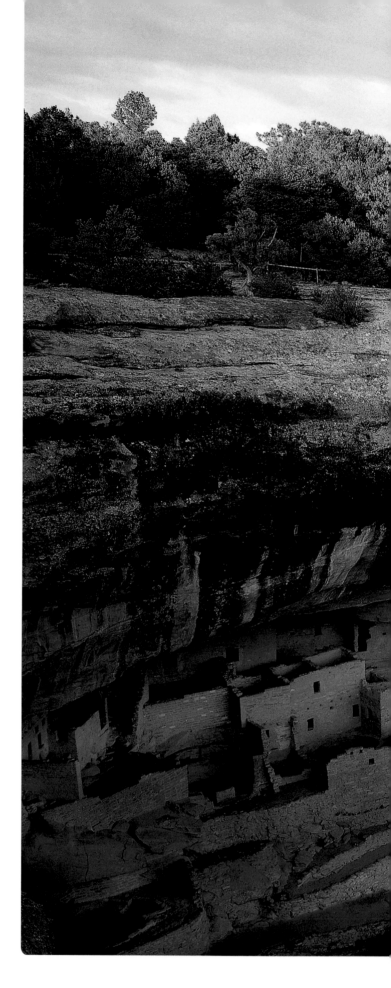

This painting inside the four-story section of Cliff Palace is remarkably well preserved. Many Ancestral Puebloan designs are geometric figures or patterns painted on a reddish-brown or off-white background. There is no written record to explain what they mean. Some of them may be symbolic or merely decoration in a living room. Regardless of their purpose, they are a tribute to the artistic talent of the Ancestral Puebloans.

GEORGE H. H. HUEY

TOM DANIELSEN

What a thrill it must have been for the cowboys who discovered Cliff Palace on that winter day in 1888. Nestled in a huge alcove, the dwelling contains 150 rooms and 23 kivas, housing around 100 people during the 1200s. Think about what a bustling community it was! Major stabilization has been done to front sections of the dwelling, but some of the finest walls remain intact. Rooms average 6 by 8 feet in size, with smaller rooms used mainly as storage areas.

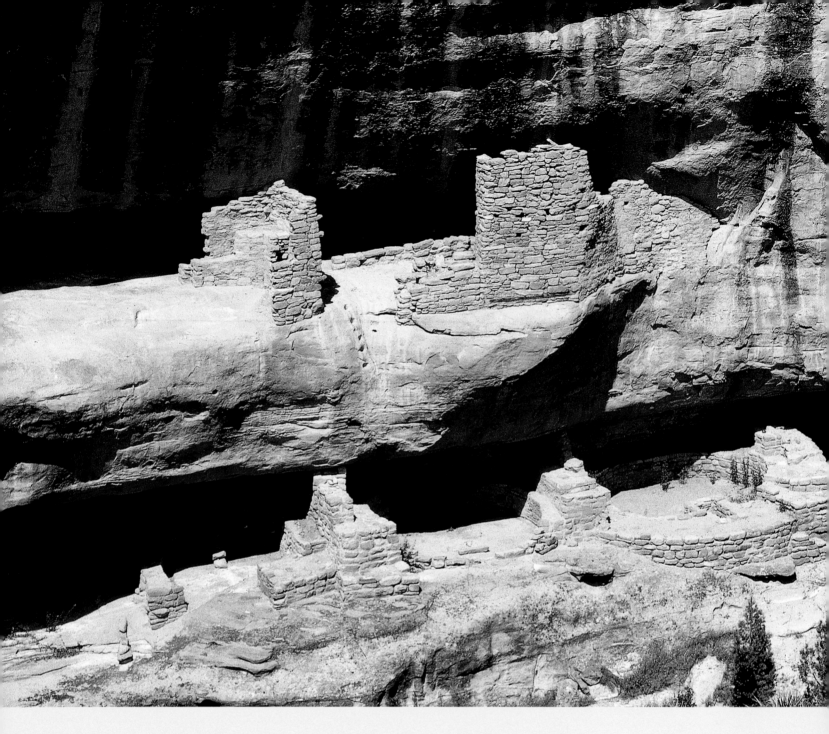

New Fire House

New Fire House, located adjacent to Fire Temple in Fewkes Canyon, contains 20 rooms and 3 Kivas. It is unusual for a dwelling so small to have that many kivas. A close look at the alcove shows toeholds carved into the cliff leading to the upper level. Upper ledges often seem inaccessible today, but the Ancestral Puebloans built rooms two and three stories high reaching to upper levels. Ladders or toeholds served as access.

Most cliff dwellings are small, single family units rather than the large ones open to the public. Typically composed of five or six rooms, a small dwelling might have a couple of storage rooms, two or three sleeping rooms, and at least one room with a firepit for cooking. The majority of these small dwellings have no kivas. Probably people living in small alcoves went to larger ones to participate in ceremonial or religious activities. Most of these small sites also remain unexcavated. They receive periodic stabilization and are preserved for future research purposed.

The Ancestral Puebloans must have visited their neighbors in nearby canyons on a regular basis. Scrambling up and down trails was an everyday occurrence. In the process they could gather wild plants, bring water from springs, gossip with other people, and exchange pottery, jewelry, or other items they made. There must have been a sense of community even for the most isolated people.

GAIL BANDINI

Fire Temple

ELIOT COHEN

***F**ire Temple in Fewkes Canyon* is one of only two dance plaza areas in Mesa Verde. In the center of the plaza is a firepit, surrounded by two troughs that may have been foot drums for the Ancestral Puebloans. When the ceremonials were in progress, chanting voices probably resonated throughout the canyon.

Balcony House

Although originally called Brownstone Front, the present name, Balcony House, seems more appropriate. The balcony in the first courtyard is beautifully preserved. From it the Ancestral Puebloans could work, have a view of Soda Canyon, and watch their children all at the same time.

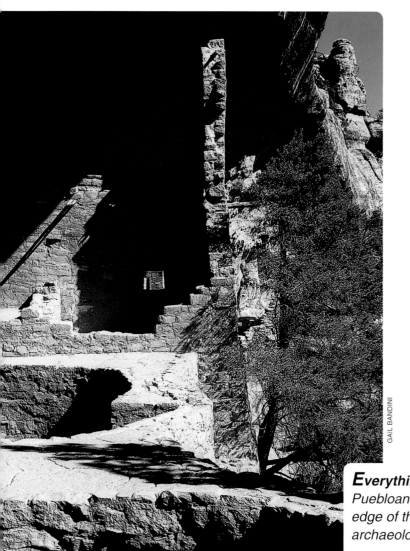

Examining the mortar between sandstone blocks reveals small chinking stones inserted into the mud. They are prominent in much original cliff-dwelling construction, and stabilization crews duplicate the effect when repairs are necessary. As a finishing touch the Ancestral Puebloans put a coating of plaster over the stones and mortar.

Everything about Balcony House was precarious for the Ancestral Puebloans. When the kivas were roofed, you could walk right off the edge of the cliff. It looks more defensive than other dwellings, yet archaeologists have no idea what the problems were.

The Ancestral **Puebloans** were **thrilled** to see the **First** signs of **Spring**

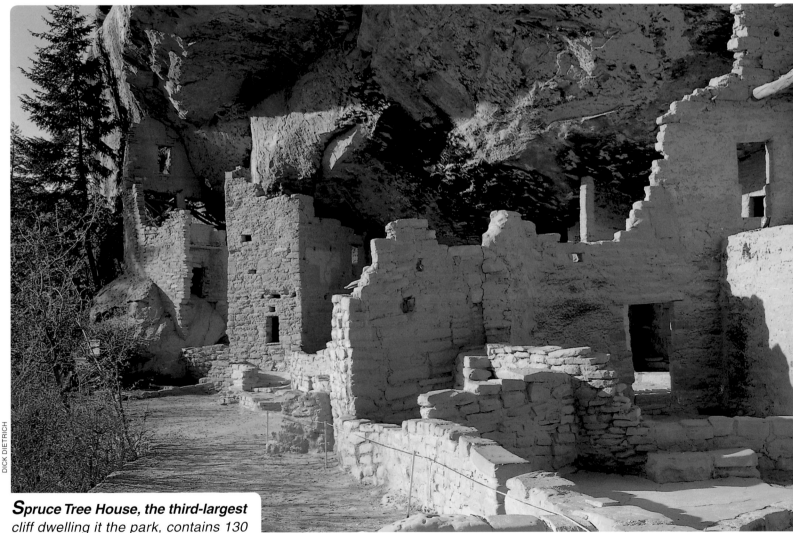

DICK DIETRICH

***S**pruce Tree House, the third-largest* cliff dwelling it the park, contains 130 rooms and 8 kivas. Visitors notice extensive smoke blackening on the roof of the alcove and wonder what it was like for the 54 - 90 occupants who inhaled so much smoke. No doubt the Ancestral Puebloans were thrilled to see the first sights of spring return each year.

***O**verleaf:* Square Tower House offers one of the most picturesque settings in Mesa Verde.
Photo by John P. George

The Ute people knew about the existence of houses in the cliffs, but did not go there because "when spirits of the dead are disturbed, then you die too."

Historic Mesa Verde

Grinding bins at Cliff Palace.
Feeding this large community required virtually an industry of grain harvesting, grinding and storing grain for the entire year. Rocks were shaped to form for this work. Mesa Verde must have been a busy place.

BRUCE HUCKO

If Mesa Verde has a fascinating prehistoric chronology, it has an equally intriguing historic one. Exactly how soon other people entered the area after the Ancestral Puebloans left is a good question. The earliest evidence of the Utes, Navajos, or Apaches arriving is in the later 1400s. Yet none of these groups moved onto the mesa tops or into the alcoves. The Ute people knew about the existence of houses in the cliffs, but did not go there because "when the spirits of the dead are disturbed, then you die too." Cultural tradition played a definite role in how they viewed the "ancient ones."

EARLY EXPLORATION PERIOD

Spanish accounts record a party passing through the Mesa Verde region in 1765. Then in 1776, the famous Dominguez-Escalante expedition explored north of the park, camping for a while near Dolores, Colorado. Somewhere along the line, the Spanish named the area Mesa Verde, a term meaning "green table". Today, visitors coming into the park look up and see the fairly flat, lush, green tableland.

For the next 100 years Mesa Verde remained essentially an unknown entity. Isolated references to dwellings do appear, and some trappers, miners, and explorers even wandered into a few canyons. For example, one cliff dwelling contains a name and an 1861 date. However, even though these people saw cliff dwellings, their interest was concentrated on mineral wealth. It remained for pioneer photographer William Henry Jackson in 1874 to enter Mancos Canyon and take the first photograph of a cliff dwelling, Two Story House, to begin publicizing the area and break the silence

The highlight of the Chapin Mesa Museum for many visitors is seeing the five dioramas depicting time periods in Mesa Verde prehistory. Each diorama concentrates on a separate aspect of architectural achievement. The Spruce Tree House diorama chronicles the Classic Pueblo Period from A.D. 1100 to 1300. Visitors are especially interested in the history of the dioramas—how they were made and who was involved in their creation. Each figure is so meticulously created it appears they were made by machine, but this was not the case. They were constructed by the mid-1930s to the early 1940s, mostly by park employees with the help of crewmembers from the Civilian Conservation Corps (CCC) camps that were in the park at the time. (This project was only one of many in the park that involved the CCC.)

DISCOVERY OF THE CLIFF DWELLINGS

In 1880, a restless Benjamin Wetherill moved his wife, five sons, and one daughter to Mancos, Colorado, to establish the Alamo cattle ranch. The family befriended the local Ute people, grazing their cattle in Mancos Canyon during the winter months. They heard about houses in the cliffs from Ute friends. In their spare time, the cowboys journeyed up the canyons looking for stray cattle and anything else of interest. On a fateful day in December 1888, Richard Wetherill and his brother-in-law, Charlie Mason, entered what they later called Cliff Palace, Spruce Tree House, and Square Tower House. Historical research shows that other people had entered the sites earlier, but the Wetherills took an immediate interest in telling the world about them.

As time passed, the Wetherills busied themselves taking collections out of the cliff dwellings and guiding tourists into the sites. The Alamo Ranch became a prominent tourist destination. Benjamin Wetherill wrote to the Smithsonian Institution to see if they would like to buy an artifact collection and asked for guidance in exploring the sites. Unfortunately, since the Smithsonian was short on funds, it passed up the opportunity. Meanwhile, the Wetherills packed up artifacts for promotional purposes, displaying them in cities across the country.

When Gustaf Nordenskiold searched for relics in Mesa Verde in 1891, he stored his camera equipment in a dwelling on what he called Wetherill Mesa. This dwelling, Kodak House, remains unexcavated and is only viewed from an overlook. It contains 70 or more rooms build on two levels and faces Rock Canyon to the west. One wonders whether Nordenkiold realized how important his photography would be in documenting a site and publicizing the area.

In **1892** Virginia Donaghe **McClurg** became almost a **one-woman** *bandwagon* in creating **Mesa Verde** National Park

KENT & DONNA DANNEN

News spread about the cliff dwellings. In June 1891, a Swedish tourist named Gustaf Nordenskiold decided that he wanted to see them personally. He had a scientific background and was enthralled by the ancient relics. He not only did the first scientific excavation work in the dwellings, but he also wrote one of the first books about the area, The Cliff Dwellers of the Mesa Verde. Nordenskiold created local resentment by shipping a collection of the discovered artifacts back to Sweden when he left Colorado. His legacy remains in the photographs he took and the research he conducted.

THE CREATION OF A PARK

A "New York Graphic" correspondent, Virginia Donaghe McClurg, visited Mesa Verde in 1892. She became almost a one-woman bandwagon to preserve the cliff dwellings and create a park out of them. Intensive lobbying began when her promotional efforts stimulated the endorsement of the Colorado Federation of Women's Clubs. By 1900, she incorporated the Colorado Cliff Dwellings Association with herself as regent. Lucy Peabody, a savvy Washington socialite, also took up the cause. Since the cliff dwellings were on Ute Reservation land, these women worked with the Utes toward a land agreement.

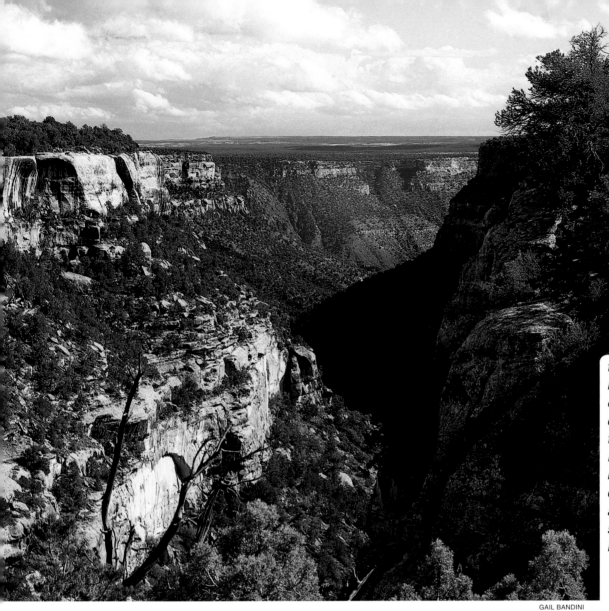

This view of Cliff Canyon is taken from near Sun Temple where Fewkes Canyon enters into Cliff Canyon. In this vicinity is the largest concentration of cliff dwellings anywhere in the park. What an incredible assortment of sites caught the cowboys' eyes when they first arrived. Fewkes excavated many of the sites during the years 1915 and 1920, and the small canyon bears his name.

GAIL BANDINI

Victorian women were not in the vanguard of national politics, but through their efforts Congress passed and President Theodore Roosevelt signed a bill creating Mesa Verde National Park on June 29, 1906.

PRESERVATION TAKES PRECEDENCE

Even though there was no adequate road into the park, cliff-dwelling preservation took precedence in the first few years. Jesse Walter Fewkes, working for the Smithsonian Institution, excavated 16 different sites in Mesa Verde, starting with Spruce Tree House in 1908. During the summer of 1909, Fewkes excavated and stabilized Cliff Palace. Later he worked at Far View and Sun Temple. In the course of this work, Fewkes also gave the first campfire programs in the National Park Service.

Probably the most influential figure in Mesa Verde National Park's history was Jesse Nusbaum. He originally came to the park in 1907 to survey and photograph sites. In 1910, he excavated and stabilized Balcony House. From 1921 to 1931, as superintendent, he transformed a struggling operation into an effectively administered park. It was Nusbaum's design which became the architectural style for the Chapin Mesa Museum and other headquarters buildings. He even established the first interpretive programs such as conducting guided tours of the ruins.

In 1913, the first wagons drove all the way from Mancos to Spruce Tree House, and by 1914 the first cars traveled this new road. This was a major breakthrough in encouraging more visitors to enter the park. There are still tales about one section of the road called the "Knife Edge." It was so steep and precarious that it was finally abandoned in 1957, when a tunnel was constructed as a shorter and safer route to Chapin Mesa.

No visitor can leave Mesa Verde without seeing examples of work done by the Civilian Conservation Corps. Several CCC camps were set up in the park in 1934. Enrollees built everything from a water system to trails to the Chapin Mesa Museum dioramas. Without their labor the park would not be what it is today.

Long House

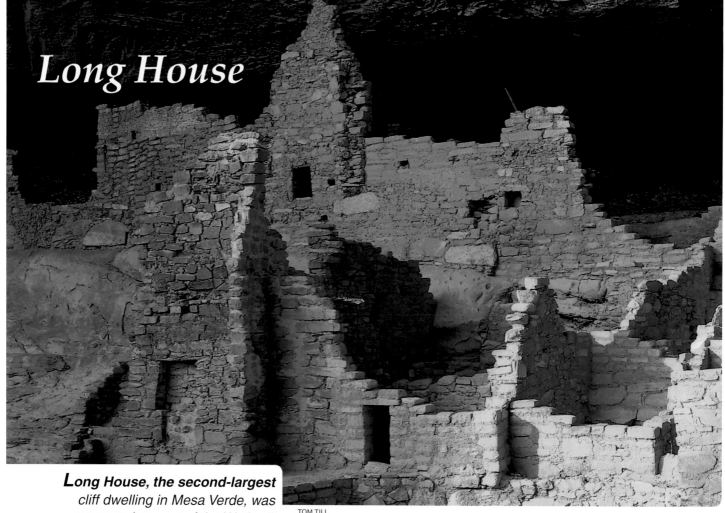

Long House, the second-largest cliff dwelling in Mesa Verde, was excavated as part of the Wetherill Mesa Archeological Project from 1958 to 1963. The long alcove provides one of the most active springs in the park. Moisture-laden moss still coats the back area, where visitors can see hollowed out potholes used for water collection. The 150-175 residents built around 150 rooms and 21 kivas in the alcove. They also constructed a great kiva or dance plaza similar to Fire Temple on Chapin Mesa. Because the dwelling has a southern exposure, it receives ample sunlight during winter months. All of these advantages must have been important to the Ancestral Puebloans who lived here.

This building houses the National Park Service *administrative offices. It is one of several buildings in the historic district built it the 1920s and early 1930s. Each building was architecturally designed to blend in with the cliff-dwelling motif.*

An Ambitious Scientific Investigation

From 1958 to 1963, the National Park Service, in conjunction with the National Geographic Society, inaugurated the most ambitious scientific investigation of Mesa Verde to date. This was the Wetherill Mesa Archeological Project, an attempt to survey, excavate, and stabilize mesa-top and cliff-dwelling sites as well as conduct other laboratory research. Long House and Step House were opened to the public as a result of this project. Archaeological investigation alone cost more than $1 million—an incredible amount of money for that time period!

These are only a few of the significant events in the history of Mesa Verde. Archaeological research continues, and stabilization efforts to keep sites in good repair are ongoing projects. To this day, Mesa Verde is the only national park set aside to protect the works of people—a tribute to its creators.

SUGGESTED READING

Multiple Authors. *The Mesa Verde Centennial Series.* Durango, Colorado: The Durango Herald Small Press, 2005, 2006.

Smith, Duane A. *Mesa Verde National Park: Shadows of the Centuries.* Lawrence, Kansas: University Press of Kansas, 1988.

Smith, Jack E. *Mesas, Cliffs, and Canyons.* Mesa Verde Museum Association, Inc., 1987.

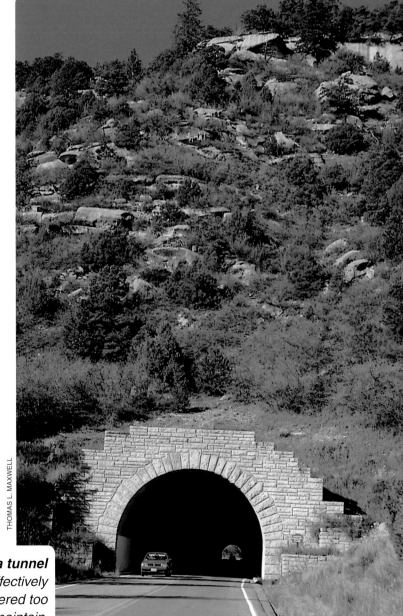

In 1957, Park Service employees constructed a tunnel *from Morefield Canyon to Prater Canyon, thereby effectively bypassing a section of the entrance road considered too treacherous to maintain.*

THOMAS L. MAXWELL

This kiva, built around A.D. 1075, is associated with one of the villages at Site 16 on the Mesa Top loop. *It is larger in diameter than many, and contains eight pilasters, or roof supports, rather than the usual six. Most kivas had a good ventilation system. When a fire was built, fresh air was drawn down the ventilator shaft (the hole in the sidewall) circling around the kiva, and smoke rose through the central opening in the roof.*

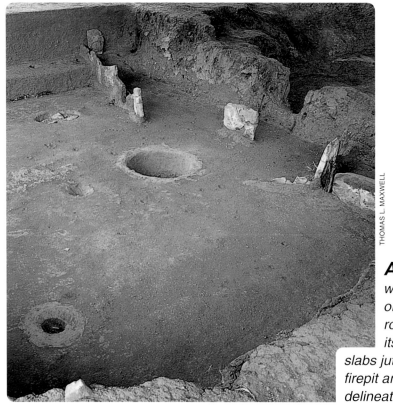

THOMAS L. MAXWELL

Access to most pithouses *was through an opening in the roof or via an antechamber—a small room connected to the pithouse itself. In this example, the stone slabs jutting out from either side of the firepit are called wing walls and help delineate the cooking area.*

Step House on Wetherill Mesa is significant because it is one of the few cliff dwellings where visitors can see both Basketmaker and Pueblo occupations. A prehistoric staircase leading to the mesa top gives the dwelling its name. Jesse Nusbaum partially excavated the site in 1926, and the remainder was excavated as part of the Wetherill Mesa Project.

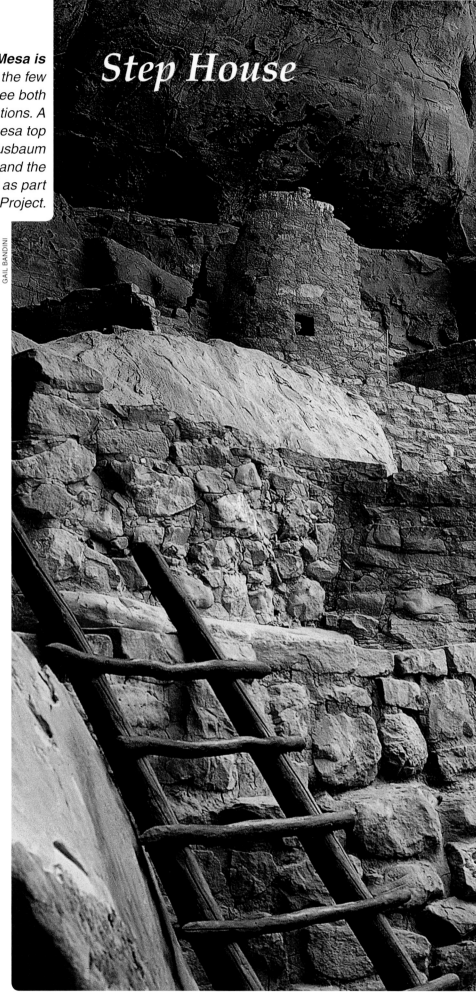

Step House

GAIL BANDINI

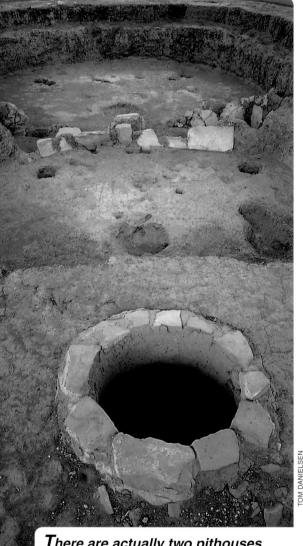

TOM DANIELSEN

There are actually two pithouses shown here. The smaller one is front overlaps the earlier one dated A.D. 674. It was characteristic of Mesa Verde pithouses to be dug deeper the later years. You can easily distinguish the two firepits and the potholes that were for logs supporting the roofs.

Most Mesa Verde canyons **were** formed by water erosion millions of years ago. The canyons are like fingers running north/south toward the Mancos River. Cliff Canyon is typical of side canyons where cliff dwellings are found in the upper band of sandstone. Lush vegetation in the canyon bottom makes walking difficult but is good browse for animals inhabiting the area. Access to the mesa top can be precarious, but the Ancestral Puebloans knew exactly how to take advantage of this canyon environment.

LARRY ULRICH

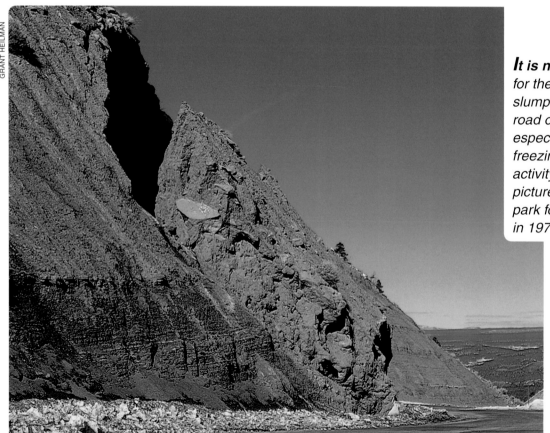

GRANT HEILMAN

It is not uncommon for the shale slopes to slump onto the entrance road of Mesa Verde, especially during spring freezing and thawing activity. The slump pictured here closed the park for an entire month in 1979 before major reinforcement made the road safe to travel again.

Geologic Forces

From Montezuma Valley Overlook visitors get a panoramic view of where the notorious Knife Edge Road used to be. This road edged along the cliff face where all sorts of problems happened when the shale began to slide. At unexpected moments, sandstone boulders tumbled down on the road. If visitors are afraid of the road today—it is not the nightmare it once was!

AILEEN MAXWELL

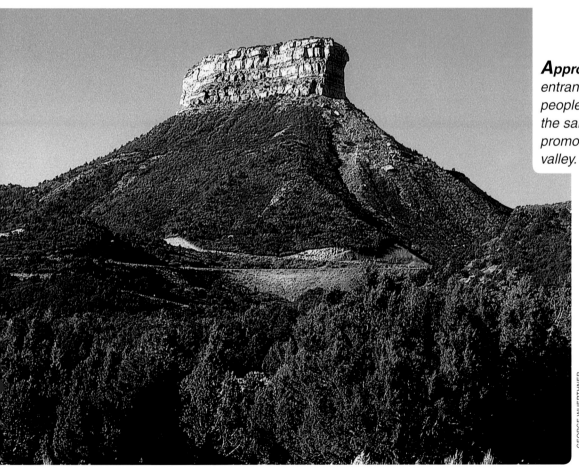

Approaching the park entrance the first glimpse people have is Point Lookout, the sandstone-capped shale promontory looming over the valley. Actually, the elevation at the entrance (about 6,900 feet) is the same as it is at the cliff dwellings. You rise to 8,500 feet at Park Point and then drop to 7,000 feet again.

GEORGE WUERTHNER

*The lucky visitor who arrives in May or June
when wildflowers are prolific sees
splashes of red, blue, yellow, and white
scattered across the mesa as it seems to
come alive with these floral displays*

Nature's Prolific Preserve

Climatically, Mesa Verde is a semi-arid region with an average rainfall of about 18 inches—just sufficient for dryland farming. Summer temperatures rise to the mid-90s (Fahrenheit), while in winter the thermometer rarely drops much below zero. With a frost-free growing season of around 150 days, and mesa-top elevations ranging from 7,000 to 8,000 feet, Mesa Verde provides good habitat for farmers as well as special niches for diverse plants and animals.

HABITAT COMMUNITIES

Recent wildfires have changed the landscape considerably, but the higher northern section of the park used to be covered by the mountain shrub community. Here Gambel oak, serviceberry, mountain mahogany, and cliff fendlerbush, interspersed with varieties of grasses, proliferated, while stands of Douglas fir nestled in sheltered side canyons of the north escarpment. Pinyon juniper forests covered the mesa tops and canyon slopes throughout the park. The Ancestral Puebloans used these trees for construction materials and firewood.

From overlooks on the Mesa Top and Cliff Palace/Balcony House Loop Roads, visitors could see deep canyon bottoms with a conspicuous absence of trees. The gray-green color of these canyon bottoms indicated dense growths of vegetation, including sagebrush, greasewood, saltbush, tomatillo, and prickly-pear cactus. All of this growth made "Mesa Verde" a very appropriate name for the park.

FLORA AND FAUNA

The lucky visitor who arrives in May or June when wildflowers are prolific sees splashes of red, blue, yellow, and white scattered across the mesa as it seems to come alive with these floral displays.

JOHN P. GEORGE

***Any park visitor who arrives from late August to** early October sees a canopy of golden-blooming rabbitbrush along the road.*

The Diversity of flora and fauna in the park is amazing

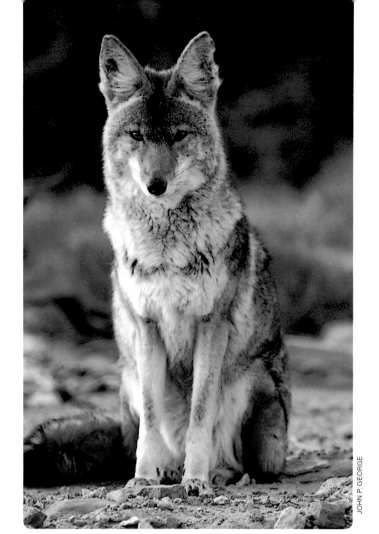

JOHN P. GEORGE

Coyotes are a familiar sight sauntering along roadways hunting for mice and rabbits. They dash into the pinyon/juniper forest at the sight of a car, only to reemerge and continue their search after the car passes.

Biologists estimate that as many as 1,500 mule deer graze in the park. Their favorite food is the antelope bitterbrush which is plentiful in the headquarters area. During harsh winter months the deer move to lower elevations in surrounding valleys.

HUGH P. SMITH JR.

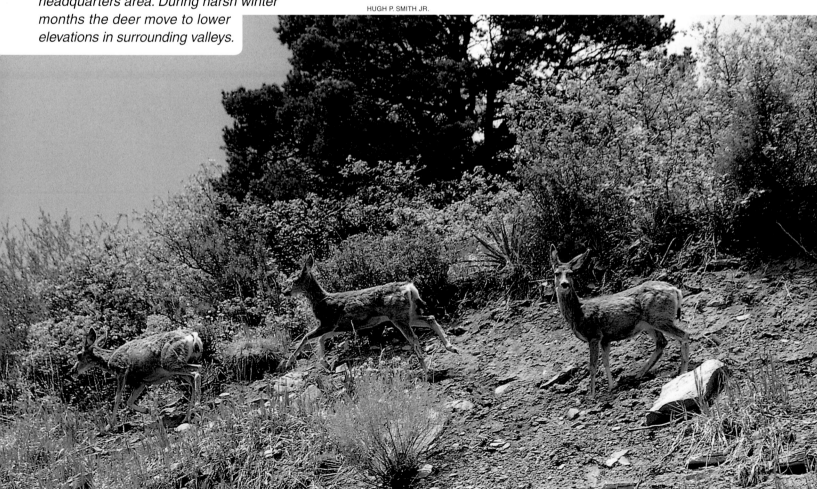

Although the Mesa Verde vegetation is home to a wide variety of animals, mule deer are the most common. They browse so consistently in Morefield Campground and the Far View Lodge areas that nearly every visitor gets a close look at them. There is a small resident herd of elk, and an occasional black bear delights an observant visitor. Less frequently seen large mammals are the gray fox, badger, bobcat, and bighorn sheep.

During the summer months both broad-tailed and black-chinned hummingbirds breed in the park, using the same nests year after year.

Year-round residents like the Steller's jay raucously scold anyone who disturbs them in picnic areas or along trails to the cliff dwellings.

RESIDENT BIRDS AND OTHER CRITTERS

The most commonly seen birds are lustrous black ravens, raucously calling to one another or soaring overhead. Other year-round residents include scrub and Steller's jays, plain titmice, mountain chickadees, white-breasted nuthatches, and golden eagles. In 1990, the park reintroduced wild turkeys which have flourished in the Morefield and Prater Canyon areas. The truly dedicated bird watcher might even spy a peregrine falcon along the cliffs of the north escarpment.

Most visitors won't see any snakes during their visit to the park. In late summer and early fall, visitors report tarantulas crossing the road or along a trail. While they may appear ferocious, they are really very docile creatures.

Archaeological excavation reveals that animal and plant species of today are the same as those living in Mesa Verde in prehistoric times. Refuse mounds contain an abundance of animal and bird bones, some of which were fashioned into tools. The diversity of flora and fauna in the park is amazing. No wonder the Ancestral Puebloans lived for so long in what appears to be such a marginal environment!

Around sunset in the Spruce Tree House vicinity 50-100 turkey vultures soar overhead, coming to rest in Douglas fir trees for the night.

Visitors regularly spot golden-mantled ground squirrels filling their pouches in Morefield Campground. In cliff dwelling areas chipmunks scurrying from place to place are more prominent, but both critters are a delight of children to watch.

ROBERT & JEAN POLLOCK

JOHN P. GEORGE

Visitors occasionally see a bull snake as they walk the path to one of the cliff dwellings. These non-poisonous snakes are hunting for mice and other critters, but they do not like being disturbed. They will sometimes coil like a rattlesnake and hiss to scare people away.

SUGGESTED READING

ELMORE, FRANCIS H. *Shrubs and Trees of the Southwest Uplands.* Globe, Arizona: Southwest Parks and Monuments Association, 1976.

DODGE, NATT N. *Flowers of the Southwest Deserts.* Tucson, Arizona: Southwest Parks and Monuments Association, 1985.

FISHER, CHRIS C. *Birds of the Rocky Mountains.* Edmonton, Alberta, Canada: Lone Pine Publishing, 1997.

THOMAS L. MAXWELL

Beautiful turquoise- and-gold collared lizards often pose for photographic enthusiasts going on tours. The larger, more colorful male stands out prominently compared to the female.

Useful Plants

The pinyon pine and Utah juniper forest prospers throughout most of the park. These hardy trees are drought resistant, thriving where moisture is minimal. Every few years pinyons produce a crop of edible nuts highly prized for their flavor and caloric value—about 5,000 per pound! Native Americans eagerly gather the nuts, but they have to beat small animals and birds to them. Pinyon pitch, the resinous gum, was used to waterproof baskets. The bluish-gray juniper berries make tangy flavoring, but they have a biting, pungent taste when taken directly from the trees. The shaggy juniper bark makes excellent bedding and was probably used for diapers by the Ancestral Puebloans.

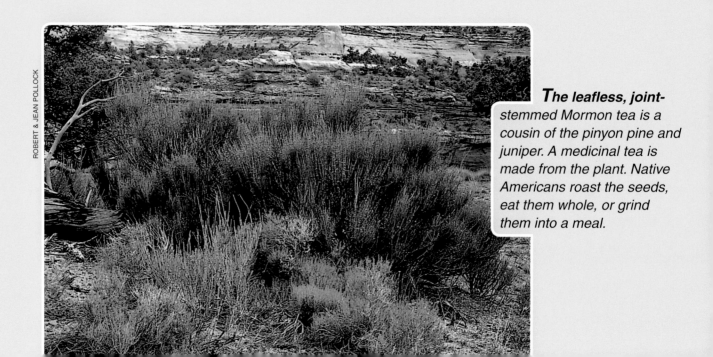

The leafless, joint- stemmed Mormon tea is a cousin of the pinyon pine and juniper. A medicinal tea is made from the plant. Native Americans roast the seeds, eat them whole, or grind them into a meal.

Growing park-wide, broad-leaved yucca was one of the most useful plants for the Ancestral Puebloans. Fibers produced cordage, sandals, leggings, and aprons. The cream-colored flowers made tasty salad or pot herbs. The banana-like fruits were eaten raw or cooked and dried as cakes.

NATIONAL PARK SERVICE

GERHARD SCHAUSS

Some prehistoric sites are covered with big sagebrush, telling archaeologists where to excavate. These gray-green shrubs commonly grow in deep canyon bottoms or on the mesa tops. They are boiled with alum to produce a green dye, and a tea from the leaves was an emetic.

Showy prickly-pear flowers bloom in June, later producing edible fruit that is sweet and gelatinous. Prickly-pear pads can be eaten raw after the spines are removed by rubbing or roasting. Scientific analysis showed that the Ancestral Puebloans ate the pads despite the bristles.

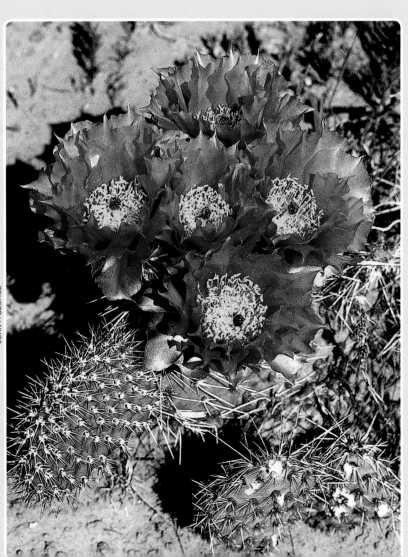

JOHN P. GEORGE

– 41 –

Fire   and ...

NPS PHOTO

Intense fire during extreme drought creates its own *unusual weather pattern. A smoke plume thousands of feet high causes erratic winds to push a wall of flame across the mesa top, igniting everything in its path. This aggressive fire behavior can only be stopped by rain or running out of fuel.*

BRUCE HUCKO

Recent park *fires affected both the archaeological and natural resources. In 2002, fire scorched all of the vegetation surrounding Cedar Tree Tower, yet the site escaped major damage.*

Recovery

Fire—A Force of Nature

Natural fire has always been a part of the Mesa Verde story, but for years the National Park Service artificially controlled fire by suppression activities. Hazardous fuels built up over time, and a prolonged drought cycle brought massive lightning strikes, igniting large wildfires. From 1989 to 2003, over 50% of Mesa Verde National Park's acreage burned.

Wildfires cause damage to the park's resources through oxidation of the sandstone rock, spalling or flaking of the rock surface, and erosion resulting from the lack of vegetation. One major panel of petroglyphs (images carved on sandstone) suffered extensive damage from spalling. A positive result of the fires was the discovery of several hundred new archaeological sites exposed when the vegetation burned.

Fire research has shown that proactive concepts such as prescribed burns and thinning dense pinyon/juniper forests help make a healthier situation. Burned Area Emergency Response (BAER) teams have been organized by the Department of the Interior to rehabilitate areas impacted by fire. Using these monitoring and research devices, Mesa Verde National Park hopes to better protect its cultural and natural resources in the future.

The positive effects of fire include increased soil fertility and rapid plant regeneration. Plants such as Gambel oak, broad-leaf yucca, and many grasses sprout new shoots from charred ground as soon as sufficient moisture reaches their roots. Pinyon pine trees take much longer to recover. Since it may be 300 years before new forests emerge, the Mesa Verde landscape will remain a patchwork appearance throughout our lifetime.

FIRE a much *needed resource,* inflicts **DAMAGE** but also *brings* **NEW LIFE!**

What a marvelous feeling to stand at Park Point
and look off for miles in every direction
with the same perspective as the
Ancestral Puebloans had hundreds of years ago.

A Look to the Future

Because of its significance as a cultural preserve, Mesa Verde National Park, in 1978, was one of the first areas designated as a World Heritage Site. This distinction has since been shared by many National Park Service areas, but few places are so intensively visited by Europeans or other international groups.

Mesa Verde is a unique area set aside to protect almost 5,000 archaeological sites. By guarding these cultural contributions, we are also preserving endangered plant species, threatened wildlife, and panoramic views of the American Southwest. What a marvelous feeling to stand at Park Point and look off for miles in every direction with the same perspective as the Ancestral Puebloans had hundreds of years ago.

PRESERVING PRICELESS ARTIFACTS

Given society's emphasis on material wealth, priceless artifacts such as pottery and basketry are threatened by the artifact hunter who is only interested in them for their dollar value. So many areas are being ravaged by this greed. Laws such as

With its location directly behind the Chapin Mesa Museum, Spruce Tree House is often the first cliff dwelling visitors see. It is also the only dwelling open on a year round basis. The spring at the head of the box canyon provided a good water supply for its inhabitants.

TOM DANIELSEN

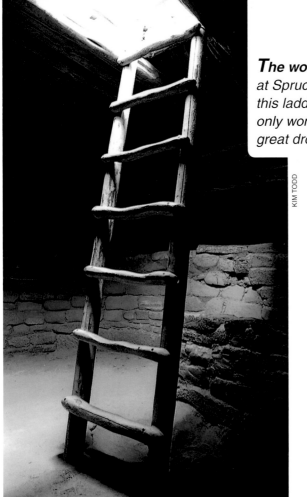

The wood ladder reaches to the sky from the floor of this kiva at Spruce Tree House. Imagine the tribal members descending this ladder into their important ceremonial happenings. We can only wonder today how much must have been discussed when the great drought hit in the late 1200's. Were the gods angry?

the Archaeological Resources Protection Act are only partially successful in controlling the plundering of America's archaeological sites.

Mesa Verde is an example of foresight in artifact preservation. Its 52,080 acres are safeguarded by national park status. Park rangers try to impress on visitors the importance of leaving potsherds or other artifacts where they find them. Children are thrilled to spot a potsherd and know that it is hundreds of years old. They are more likely to look at it and leave it where they found it if a ranger explains how other children can have the same experience. Children truly do learn to appreciate what national parks provide, carrying that message into adulthood.

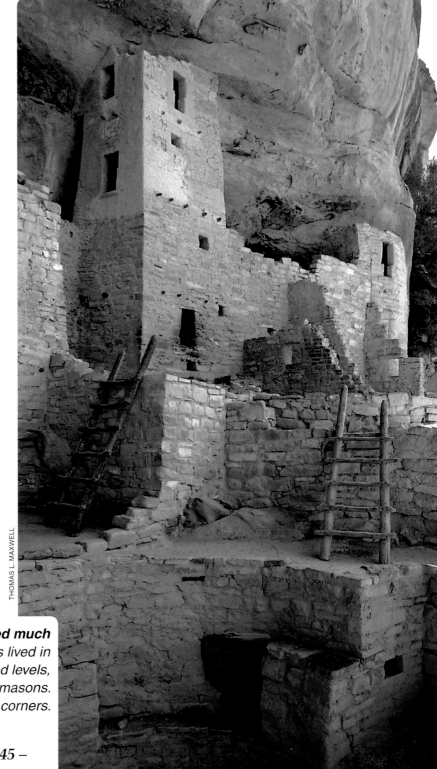

The four-story "tower" area of Cliff Palace looked much like an apartment house when the Ancestral Puebloans lived in the dwelling. Cliff Palace was built on various terraced levels, illustrating the architectural skills of these stone-age masons. Visitors marvel at the tall, straight walls with their precise corners.

All About Mesa Verde National Park

Mesa Verde Museum Association

Mesa Verde Museum Association (MVMA) is a private, nonprofit organization that was established in 1930 to support the mission of the National Park Service and Mesa Verde National Park. Through an active publishing program and the operation of retail bookstores in Mesa Verde National Park, MVMA offers educational and interpretive materials to our visitors. Proceeds from the sale of these items support interpretive, educational, and research programs at Mesa Verde. MVMA's goal is to enhance public understanding of the importance of protecting the cultural and natural resources at Mesa Verde National Park and all public lands. For more information please visit our on-line bookstore at www.mesaverde.org.

GOLDEN-MANTLED GROUND SQUIRREL   ROBERT & JEAN POLLOCK

MESA VERDE
Junior Ranger

What is the Junior Ranger Program?

Adventure—is what you will have when visiting Mesa Verde National Park, while achieving your goal of becoming a Junior Ranger. Take a tour of one of the cliff houses, and learn how the Ancestral Puebloans built these magnificent homes. See how they lived, and what they did from day to day. Find out what the Ancestral Puebloans used for hunting, and what they wore and ate. Ask a ranger for the Junior Ranger Application from any of the ranger stations, and complete the selected activities according to your age. Then return to a ranger to take the Junior Ranger pledge and receive your Junior Ranger badge. **Wear it with pride!**

US 160

Denny Lake

MONTEZUMA VALLEY

N

Park Entrance Station

Point Lookout
8417 ft
2569 m

MANCOS VALLEY

US 160

Mud Creek

Mancos River

The Knife Edge
8290 ft
2527 m

Mancos Valley Overlook

Morefield Village

Montezuma Valley Overlook

EAST RIM

Tunnel

Park Point
8571 ft
2621 m

NORTH RIM

Wetherill Mesa Road

MESA VERDE NATIONAL PARK

EAST CANYON

Far View Lodge

Far View Terrace

Far View Visitor Center
8040 ft
2452 m

SODA CANYON

Mummy Lake

Far View Ruins
7630 ft
2341 m

PRATER CANYON

MOREFIELD CANYON

MANCOS CANYON

LONG SPUR

WEST FORK

EAST FORK

LONG CANYON

WEST FORK

WEST FORK

EAST FORK

ROCK CANYON

UTE MOUNTAIN INDIAN RESERVATION

HORSE CANYON

WILDHORSE MESA

NAVAJO CANYON

WICKIUP CANYON

SPRUCE CANYON

CHAPIN MESA

SODA CANYON

PARK MESA

SCHOOL SECTION CANYON

MOCCASIN MESA

MOCCASIN CANYON

WATERS CANYON

MOREFIELD MESA

WHITES MESA

BIG MESA

WHITES CANYON

WEAVER CANYON

SWIFT CANYON

Step House

Long House

Kodak House

WETHERILL MESA

ROCK CANYON

Cedar Tree Tower and Kiva

Prehistoric farming terraces

Museum

Ruins Road

Spruce Canyon Trail

Spruce Tree House

Park Headquarters

Petroglyph Point Trail

Petroglyph Point

Sun Temple

New Fire House

Early Pithouse

Cliff Palace

Square Tower House

Oak Tree House

Late Pithouses and Early Pueblo Ruins

Pueblo Ruins

Balcony House

House of Many Windows

UTE MOUNTAIN INDIAN RESERVATION

Mancos River

MANCOS CANYON

LEWIS MESA

Mesa Verde National Park

Park elevations range from 6200 feet in deep canyon bottoms to 8500 feet at Park Point.
Temperatures drop to zero degrees Fahrenheit in winter and rise to the mid-90's in summer.

US 6

COLORADO

UTAH

I-70

I-70

US 191

Denver

I-25

Arches N.P.

Canyonlands N.P.

Capitol Reef N.P.

Natural Bridges N.M.

Black Canyon of the Gunnison N.M.

Mesa Verde N.P.

Great Sand Dunes N.M.

US 50

Glen Canyon Dam

US 160

Canyon de Chelly N.M.

Durango

US 666

US 84

US 89

ARIZONA

US 191

Farmington

NEW MEXICO

I-25

Santa Fe

Petrified Forest N.P.

I-40

Flagstaff

US 17

Albuquerque

I-40

A Lasting Message

The Ancestral Puebloan legacy has another lasting message for modern society. In the 1200s they overused the land, depleted the timber resources, and overhunted the wildlife, just as 20th-century people have done. We hear on the news daily about critical pollution problems, ozone depletion, and overpopulation. As we look at what happened to the Ancestral Puebloans, perhaps it will be a lesson to us for the future. History does repeat itself, and Mesa Verde is a place to contemplate our wants and needs. If only one visitor in ten takes this message to heart, Mesa Verde is educating thousands of people every year. Give thanks to the Ancestral Puebloans— their spirit is still with us!

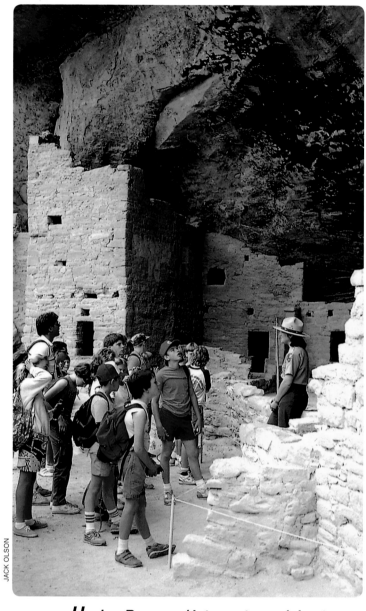

JACK OLSON

Having Rangers / Interpreters, giving tours *provide both accurate knowledge and protection of these resources.*

KC Publications has been the leading publisher of colorful, interpretive books about National Park areas, public lands, Indian lands, and related subjects for over 45 years. We have 6 active series—over 125 titles—with Translation Packages in up to 8 languages for over half the areas we cover. Write, call, or visit our web site for our full-color catalog.

Our series are:

The Story Behind the Scenery® – Compelling stories of over 65 National Park areas and similar Public Land areas. Some with Translation Packages.

in pictures... Nature's Continuing Story™ – A companion, pictorially oriented, series on America's National Parks. All titles have Translation Packages.

For Young Adventurers® – Dedicated to young seekers and keepers of all things wild and sacred. Explore America's Heritage from A to Z.

Voyage of Discovery® – Exploration of the expansion of the western United States.

Indian Culture and the Southwest – All about Native Americans, past and present.

Calendars – For National Parks in dramatic full color, and a companion Color Your Own series.

**To receive our full-color catalog featuring over 125 titles—Books, Calendars, and other related specialty products:
Call (800-626-9673), fax (702-433-3420), write to the address below, or visit our web sites at www.kcpub.com and www.kcspeaks.com**

Published by KC Publications, P.O. Box 3615, Wickenburg, AZ 85358

Inside back cover: *Imagine families living here, this was their home and way of protection. Photo by Bruce Hucko.*

Back cover: *Sun Temple is a favorite spot for reliving a memorable day. Photo by Terry Donnelly.*

Created, Designed, and Published in the U.S.A.
Printed by Tien Wah Press (Pte.) Ltd, Singapore
Pre-Press by United Graphic Pte. Ltd